UNMARRIED and DEBT-FREE

UNMARRIED and DEBT-FREE

**Ten Things Every Unmarried Man and
Woman Should Know about Money**

Livia Kelly

ISBN: 978-1-7336390-0-2

Library of Congress Cataloging-in-Publication Data

Kelly, Livia
    Unmarried and Debt-Free: ten things every unmarried man and woman should know about money / Livia Kelly. – 1st ed.

1.   Business and economics - Personal finance – Money management.
2.   Self-help – Personal growth – Success. I. Title.

TXu002130004 / 2019

Disclaimer
The author of this book is not a financial counselor or professional, and you should view this information only as input from her personal application of the written material. The information and/or documents contained in this book do not constitute investment advice. The ideas, product recommendations, and strategies should never be used without first assessing your own personal and financial situation or without consulting a financial professional.

Editing and cover design by Elite Authors

Author photograph by Nicole Tyler

Printed in the United States of America

First Edition

Visit the author's website at www.liviakellyauthor.com

Table of Contents

Preface · vii

My Money Journey ·ix

Chapter 1   A Monthly Budget Is a Necessity · 1

Chapter 2   Having Good Credit Is Essential · 11

Chapter 3   You Need an Emergency Savings Fund · · · · · · · · · · · · · · · · · 16

Chapter 4   Paying Off Your Debt Is Freeing · 21

Chapter 5   Invest in Your Future· 27

Chapter 6   Things to Consider before Buying a Home · · · · · · · · · · · · · · · 33

Chapter 7   You Need Disability Insurance · 38

Chapter 8   You Also Need Life Insurance · 41

Chapter 9   Make an Impact · 43

Chapter 10   Before You Wed · 47

Let's Reflect ···51

Acknowledgments···53

Endnotes···55

Helpful Resources ···57

Preface

Everyone experiences "life events" at some point, such as health issues, the death of a loved one, a divorce, or the loss of a job. However, because most unmarried men and women are the sole income earners, when they face life events, the outcomes may be very different from those who are married. The result of the life event could cause a crisis if their finances are not in order.

During a recent five-year period, I experienced two unrelated health conditions that caused me to miss work for a long period of time due to surgery, physical rehabilitation, and recovery.

Today I am thankful and grateful to God that I am in good health. Looking back, I am truly blessed that as an unmarried person, I had developed the practice of managing my money and so did not incur any debt during or after these life events.

Whether you're divorced, widowed, or have never been married, whether you have children or no children, unmarried people are one of the fastest-growing demographics in our society.

Although a large number of Americans are finding that remaining unmarried has its advantages, there is one key area making this more difficult today than in the past, and that is money.

Here are a few facts to support this:

- There are 110.6 million unmarried people living in America age 18 and older. This group makes up 45.2 percent of all US residents age 18 and older.[1]
- Thirty-five million people live alone. They comprise 28 percent of all households.[2]

- Almost 6 in 10 unpartnered adults (58 percent) have never been married. About a fifth (21 percent) are divorced, and 14 percent are widowed.[3]
- About one-third of US children are living with an unmarried parent.[4]
- A woman reaching 65 today can expect to live on average until age 86.7 years, compared to 84.3 years for men.[5]
- Nearly two-thirds of US women ages 40–79 have already dealt with a major financial life crisis, such as a job loss, a divorce, the death of a spouse, or a serious illness.[6]
- The median household income (adjusted for household size) for partnered adults, either married or cohabiting, is $86,000. In contrast, the median household income for unpartnered adults is roughly $61,000.[7]

In addition, married couples can split the mortgage, benefit from insurance discounts, and receive tax breaks for filing jointly. And it's cheaper when two people are splitting the utility bills, the insurance bills, and all the bills that come with living somewhere. These facts are concerning; however, you can still live a satisfying life as an unmarried person if you are willing to save and manage your money.

Although there's a lot of information available about managing finances, most of it gives very little perspective on living a debt-free life as an unmarried person. As an unmarried person who has been living a life free of debt, I've decided it's time to give some insight into the key points of managing your money.

My Money Journey

How often has something happened in your life that you later realized was necessary to make you a better person? If you hadn't experienced this or walked through that, then you wouldn't be ready for the blessings that you enjoy now. God directs our steps, delights in every detail of our lives, and never takes his eyes or his hands off us. God uses the life events or trials in our lives to develop and mature us so that we can be blessings to others.

My Twenties: All about Me and Material Things

After finishing college, I relocated from Steilacoom, Washington, to Memphis, Tennessee, to become a flight attendant. This had been my goal since my freshman year of high school.

Prior to this, I worked my way through college as a senior sales specialist at a local department store, and I was able to save $5,000, which paid my expenses during my flight attendant training and relocation to Memphis. Because I am overly independent, I didn't want my parents to pay for anything at this point in my life.

As you can guess, I spent the $5,000 rather quickly. When I moved to Memphis, I had to take a taxi to and from the airport until another flight attendant, who had been flying for a while, took me to get my driver's license and a new car. That day was a day to remember.

I still remember calling my parents and telling them all I had accomplished. My mother was shocked when I told her about the 13 percent rate of interest that I was paying for my new car, and she told me to have the car refinanced at a lower interest rate. The next morning, I did as she suggested: I contacted a credit union and secured a lower rate.

During this decade, I became a compulsive purchaser, racking up $20,000 in debt between three maxed-out credit cards and a car loan. My wake-up call came after the Persian Gulf War, which triggered a recession in America and a decline in airline passenger traffic. The airline laid off thousands of workers and implemented large pay cuts to the remaining employees.

After learning about the pay cut, I made a commitment to start making smarter financial decisions. I also came to the realization that the airline industry is highly competitive and cyclical and can be affected by several external factors, such as volatile jet fuel prices and economic uncertainty.

I started looking for ways to replace the income I had lost. A colleague introduced me to a home-based business opportunity with a top global multibillion-dollar cosmetics company. This enticed me, and within a few days, I became an independent beauty consultant. I was in my mid-twenties.

Within thirty months of starting my business, I earned my first career car and sold my old car. This, coupled with my commissions, allowed me to pay off all my debt and to replace the income I was losing due to the pay cut. By the time I was twenty-nine years old, I purchased my first home.

My Thirties: The Title-and-Status Years

Along with continuing to work as a flight attendant, I earned the title of independent sales director, where I recruited and trained hundreds of women and men in brand marketing and sales, as well as oversaw the planning and budgeting of weekly, monthly, and quarterly events. A highlight of my career was when I was recognized for ten consecutive years as one of the top independent sales directors in the nation for personal sales. I earned the use of four more career cars as well.

After purchasing my new home, I started to accumulate debt again. Around this time, I attended a leadership conference for independent sales directors, where I had the opportunity to be trained by a nationally known financial adviser and motivational speaker. After attending the conference, I made the decision to stop living paycheck to paycheck and to develop the money management skills that would keep me out of debt for good. I started reading information on managing money, and I applied the necessary steps to live a life free of debt.

In my mid-thirties, the airline industry and world were rocked by September 11, 2001, now known worldwide as 9/11. At the time, I was out of debt and saving money, which often allowed me to take company convenience leaves from flying. On September 11, 2001, I was in the middle of a three-month leave. As a result of 9/11, the airline industry saw massive financial losses due to lack of passenger demand, canceled flights, and increased expenditures for security. Most airlines were forced to renegotiate labor contracts, offer voluntary furloughs, and lay off high numbers of employees with no guarantee they would be recalled. My original three-month leave was extended to a five-year voluntary furlough.

I stayed out of debt the remainder of the decade while living on commission from my home-based business. I ended the decade with my mortgage as my only debt, and I continued to build a solid emergency savings fund.

My Forties: The Years I Learned to Be Still and Listen to God

To my surprise, the airline recalled me to return to work as a flight attendant. I was surprised because the airline had filed bankruptcy a few months earlier to restructure. However, the timing was just right; after ten years of working very hard as an independent sales director, I was losing the passion that I once had. In addition, I began to feel God directing my steps to resign. I returned to flying, and after a few months, I made the decision to resign from my sales position. Two months later, the world was affected by the Great Recession.

There are times in our lives when it may seem that God is silent, but he is never silent. What seems like silence and inactivity to us is God allowing us the opportunity to listen and to see the provisions that he has made for us by faith. God is involved in every area of our lives. However, there are times when we must be still and stop chasing after titles, status, or material things.

My mid- to late forties brought some challenges that I had never experienced in my lifetime. Up to this point, I had been very healthy. In high school, I was a three-time Washington State track champion. Although I chose not to compete in track during my college years, I continued to run and exercise throughout my twenties, thirties, and forties. I even completed the Kona Marathon.

Within a five-year period, I experienced two unrelated health conditions requiring surgery, physical therapy, and recovery. I was off work for an extended period of time. I am thankful and grateful to God and his word for bringing me through as he restored my strength and healed my body. As a result of these life events, I developed a much stronger relationship with him. And I will be forever grateful to my team of health professionals who provided exceptional care, and to my family and friends who prayed for my healing, accompanied me during my appointments and surgery, and gave me ongoing encouragement.

Another life event took place in my late forties, when I relocated to Atlanta, Georgia. Looking back, I am truly blessed that as an unmarried person, I had developed the practice of managing my money and was able to remain debt-free during and after these events.

My forties were filled with life events that reinforced the importance of budgeting, having emergency savings, being familiar with my health-care plan and other insurance, and having the right documents in place for my loved ones in case something happened to me. In my twenties and thirties, I learned to manage things on my own, but during this season, I had to listen to the whisper from God for direction. For those readers who are not believers in Christ, please understand that I am not hearing some audible voice from above when I speak of a whisper from God. Rather, it is having a feeling of peace after I have prayed and asked God for wisdom and direction in any given area of my life. This is what believers in Christ know as the Holy Spirit. I have learned when it's God's will for me to pursue something in my life, then I have peace regarding the decision. In other words, God gives direction without doubt. My forties were the years that God used to draw me closer to him.

My Fifties: Which I'm Calling My Fabulous Fifties

Today as an unmarried person in my early fifties, I am living a healthy and happy life free of debt. Like most fifty-somethings, I am working to build my retirement savings. My life experiences through the decades have allowed me to gain wisdom in all areas of my life, especially in regard to my finances.

The Benefits of Living a Debt-Free Life

There are many reasons to want to live a life free of debt. Debt leads to stress, and stress contributes to illness, heart disease, hypertension, and stroke. If you aren't in control of your finances, your stress could build toward dangerous, unhealthy levels and could even contribute to death.

Many people enjoy the feeling of achievement that creating and sticking with a budget brings, not to mention the freedom of accomplishing other goals when you're not burdened with debt.

Living a life free of debt won't ever mean getting rid of all your bills. Each month you'll still need to pay for expenses, such as your utilities, shelter, and transportation. However, living a life free of debt means that you'll be on time and up to date with all your monthly expenses and will not owe any money over and above those expenditures.

You may be asking yourself if it is really possible to live a life free of debt as an unmarried person. I know from experience that you can achieve this if you are willing to do the work to be in control of your finances and spending. When I made the decision to live a life free of debt, I had to learn to set clear goals and to keep things simple and attainable.

In the chapters of this book, I will give you practical advice about money based on my accumulated knowledge, experience, and wisdom, all of which I have applied to gain insight into managing my finances over the years.

All right, let's get started.

CHAPTER 1

A Monthly Budget Is a Necessity

When I started tracking my spending, I was very intimidated by the idea of creating a budget. I felt that it was too complicated and cumbersome for me to take on. However, after developing and using a budget for a few months, I learned that it can be as detailed or as basic as you decide to make it. Creating a monthly budget is the key to living a debt-free life.

Monthly Budget Basics

It doesn't matter if you're on a fixed income or if you're a millionaire: you still need a monthly budget because debt affects all income levels.

A monthly budget is a summary of your financial income and expenses during a given month. By documenting all your income for the month and all your expenses, you have a record for that month. When you use that information to plan ahead for the beginning of the next month, you now have a budget.

Creating a budget allows you to determine in advance whether you will have enough money to do the things you need to do or would like to do. Making a monthly budget is the most critical step in getting and staying out of debt. In fact, when I briefly got back into debt after buying my first home in my early thirties, it was the result of not making a budget.

Creating a monthly budget can be as simple as writing down your income and expenses on a sheet of paper. The goal is to track all your expenses and income on a monthly basis so that you can accurately project your needs for the next month.

Monthly Budget Benefits

- Budgeting helps you gain control of your finances.
- Budgeting helps you achieve your financial goals.
- A good budget keeps you honest. By documenting purchases, you identify gaps in your spending where you could cut back, such as the money you spend daily on a cup of coffee.
- Budgeting helps improve habits, which will prevent you from spending more money than you earn.
- A budget helps you avoid debt and improve credit. By tracking your spending and paying your bills on time, you will take the most important step toward building good credit.

How a Monthly Budget Works

1. **The simplest way to create a budget is to go online and view all your monthly billing history, or gather all your financial statements**, and create a monthly average of your spending habits from your recent pay stubs, utility bills, bank statements, credit card statements, investment accounts, and any other information that will provide the most accurate estimate regarding your income or expenses. If you're unsure or unclear about any debts, contact the appropriate customer service department right away.

2. **List all your sources of income.** If your income is in the form of a regular paycheck, then use the net income (after state and federal taxes, employer deductions, and insurance premiums). Include self-employed income as well as all other sources of income. It's important to identify the money you expect to have coming in.

3. **Create a list of monthly expenses.** You can do this by writing down a list of all the expected expenses you plan to incur over the course of the month.

This includes your rent or home mortgage, car payments, auto insurance, utilities, groceries, student loans, savings, and everything else you spend your money on.

4. **Separate your expenses into two categories: fixed and variable.** Fixed expenses are those that stay relatively the same each month. Some examples of fixed expenses are your rent or home mortgage, car payments, and internet service. Variable expenses are the type that change from month to month and include such expenses as giving, gasoline, groceries, and eating out.

5. **Calculate your monthly income and monthly expenses.** If your calculations show you have more income than expenses (a surplus), then you are living within your means, and you can use the excess (leftover) income to start paying off your debt or to achieve other financial goals. However, if your expenses are more than your income (a deficit), then you will need to adjust your variable expenses. For example, you may be spending $350 in your food budget. Instead of eating out three nights a week, you could lower your food budget by $100 per month if you ate out only two times per week. The goal is to find areas where you can reduce your variable expenses.

6. **Set realistic goals for your money.** Make a list of what you would like to accomplish with your money, both in the short term and over the long term. In the short term, you may be able to reduce spending and credit card debt quickly, but it may take years to get ready for retirement. Ask yourself, "What do I want my finances to look like in six months, one year, five years, or ten years?"

Monthly Budget Resources

There are several tools available for creating a monthly budget:

- Apps (e.g., YNAB or PocketGuard)
- Online templates (Vertex42 has a number of styles to choose from.)
- Pencil and paper
- Software (e.g., Mint or Quicken)
- Spreadsheets and manually tracking your receipts (e.g., Google Sheets Budget or Microsoft Excel)

Create Your Monthly Budget

Regardless of the monthly budget tool you decide to use, you should create a budget that uses income and expense categories. In addition, your monthly budget should note your average expense for each category as well as show a grand total for monthly income, minus total expenses, which will either show a surplus (leftover money) or a deficit.

I use some of the following categories, which are recommended by many financial experts. You should use the categories that represent areas of significance in your budget, delete those that do not, and add any important categories that may be missing.

- Income
- Charity/giving
- Children
- Clothing
- Debt
- Dependent/eldercare
- Education
- Entertainment
- Food
- Health/medical
- Housing
- Personal
- Pets
- Recreation
- Savings
- Transportation
- Travel
- Utilities

The income and expenses within each category include the following:

- **Income:** Monthly salary, interest, dividends, commissions, bonuses, tips, retirement income, cash gifts, net business income, child support/alimony
- **Charity/giving:** Tithes and offerings to church and religious organizations, charitable donations to nonprofit organizations, gifts (birthdays, anniversaries, weddings, Christmas, graduation, baby showers)

- **Children:** Childcare, diapers, clothing, sports and hobbies, allowance
- **Clothing:** Shoes, outerwear, work wear, accessories
- **Debt:** Credit cards, auto loans, student loans, home equity loans
- **Dependent/eldercare:** Home care provider, day-care center, day/summer camp
- **Education:** Adult education, children's tuition, supplies, lessons, activities
- **Entertainment:** Movie tickets, concert tickets, sporting events, miscellaneous recreation
- **Food:** Groceries, eating out, coffee and drinks
- **Health/medical:** Doctor, dentist, prescriptions, vision, dental insurance, disability insurance, health insurance, long-term care insurance, deductibles, health savings account/flexible spending, gym memberships
- **Housing:** Rent, renters insurance, mortgage (including property taxes and insurance in escrow), home maintenance, homeowner association/condo fees
- **Personal:** Discretionary spending, hair care, life insurance, identity theft insurance, legal and tax preparation, laundry and dry cleaning, subscriptions and dues, sports and hobbies, alimony and child support
- **Pets:** Food and supplies, grooming, veterinarian, pet sitting and boarding
- **Savings:** Emergency savings fund, retirement savings (Roth IRA, 401(k), 403(b), 457(b), Traditional IRA), college savings (529), stocks, bonds, vacation savings fund
- **Transportation:** Fuel, auto insurance, auto maintenance, auto registration, bus passes, train tickets, fares, tolls, auto club, miscellaneous transportation costs
- **Travel:** Vacations, airfare, hotel, car rental
- **Utilities:** Electric, gas, water, trash, cell/home phone, cable/internet, home security

It's important to track your income and expenses for the next thirty days to understand what you are actually earning and spending. It's best to work with real numbers when creating a monthly budget. I recommend that you save every receipt after every purchase, and carry something with you to track your transactions every time you receive income and every time you spend over the next thirty days. In addition, to save time when recording your expenses, you may want to note the expense category on each receipt after every purchase. For example, if you purchase a cup of coffee, you would note "food" on the receipt, or if you purchase fuel for your car, you would note "transportation" on the receipt. Stay organized by placing your receipts in an envelope or by using a receipt scanner app.

On the following pages, you will find two monthly budget worksheets. You'll notice that a budget can be very basic or very detailed. If you begin by using a complicated tool, you can quickly and easily become overwhelmed. This will likely cause you to quit before you even get started. Depending on your personality and your comfort with technology, you should select a tool that works with your routine. Basically, it all comes down to managing your money in a way that makes sense to you.

Monthly Budget for Month/Year of _____		
Income	**Planned Average**	**Actual**
Wages/salary (after taxes)		
Other income		
TOTAL MONTHLY INCOME		
Expenses	**Planned Average**	**Actual**
Giving		
Savings		
Housing		
Utilities		
Transportation		
Food		
Entertainment		
Personal		
Children/eldercare		
Pets		
Health/medical		
Debt		
TOTAL EXPENSES		
TOTAL INCOME − TOTAL EXPENSES = SURPLUS OR DEFICIT:		

Monthly Budget for Month/Year of _____						
Income Source	**Planned Average**	**Week 1**	**Week 2**	**Week 3**	**Week 4**	**Total**
TOTAL INCOME: _____ (MONTHLY AVERAGE) _____ (MONTHLY TOTAL)						
Monthly Expenses						
Giving						
Savings						
Housing						
Rent/mortgage						
▪ Insurance						
▪ Repairs/fees						
▪ Property taxes						
Utilities						
▪ Cable/satellite						
▪ Electricity						
▪ Gas						
▪ Internet						
▪ Phone						
▪ Trash						
▪ Water						
Transportation						
▪ Car insurance						
▪ Gas and oil						
▪ License/taxes						
▪ Repairs/tires						
Food/entertainment						
▪ Dining out						
▪ Groceries						
▪ Sports/hobbies						

Income Source	Planned Average	Week 1	Week 2	Week 3	Week 4	Total
Monthly Expenses (Cont.)						
Personal						
• Clothing						
• Disability insurance						
• Health insurance						
• Life insurance						
Children/eldercare						
• Home care provider						
Pets						
• Food and supplies						
Debt						
• Credit cards						
• Auto loans						
• Student loans						
TOTAL EXPENSES						
TOTAL INCOME − TOTAL EXPENSES = SURPLUS OR DEFICIT:						

Create a Monthly Average

After tracking your income and expenses for thirty days, you will want to create a monthly average for each "Income" and "Expense" category. You may find this to be challenging at first because you may be spending more than you are earning. However, each month you continue this process, you will refine your budget, which will assist you in reducing your monthly expenses.

List Your Income

List all your income in the "Income" section of your monthly budget. Many people do not receive consistent, predictable income. This is especially common for those who are self-employed or working on commission. If your income is not consistent, estimate your yearly income and divide by twelve to determine your average monthly income.

List Your Expenses

Complete and total each "Expense" category on your monthly budget. Then add them together to determine your total expenses for the month. As discussed earlier, not all expenses are consistent each month. Expenses that vary include the following:

- **Variable monthly expenses:** These can include giving, food, and utilities. Simply estimate what you spend in an average month. As you continue to use your monthly budget, you will become more accurate in projecting these expenses.
- **Expenses that do not occur every month:** These can include medical bills, auto maintenance, clothing, and travel. You will want to estimate the annual amount spent for an item and divide by twelve. For example, if you spend $600 a year in auto maintenance, set aside $50 a month to pay for repairs.

Determine Your Budget Surplus or Deficit

At the bottom of your monthly budget, subtract your "Total Expenses" from your "Total Income" to determine whether you have a surplus or deficit: total income − total expenses = surplus or deficit.

If your total income is greater than your expenses, then you have a surplus, and the leftover money can be applied to pay off your debt or to meet your other financial goals. If your expenses are greater than your income, then you have a deficit. If you have a deficit in your budget, this is an indication that it may be necessary to reduce your spending, or you may need to find additional ways to increase your monthly income.

Adjust Your Monthly Spending

As you continue to track your income and expenses, you'll discover that your monthly budget is always changing and in need of adjustments. Spending less than you earn is your main objective.

Adjusting your monthly spending will remind you to try to continue to reduce your expenses and to increase your income so that your monthly surplus will grow. Eating out less frequently, preparing your lunch, cutting the lawn instead of using a lawn service, or being more aware of the amounts of water and electricity you are using are just a few examples of how you can lower your monthly expenses.

Your first monthly budget should be simple to manage and to keep up with to help you get a handle on your finances. A budget does not have to be complicated or overly detailed. It should account for every dollar you earn and spend. Doing this will help you make smart spending choices.

Creating a budget on a monthly basis might not sound like the most enjoyable task, but it's a necessary part of keeping your finances in order and keeping you out of mounting debt.

CHAPTER 2

Having Good Credit Is Essential

W hen you think about it, you can be rich in one of two ways: either in how much you have or in how little you want. Much of the recent debt crisis has been caused by our failure to be satisfied with enough.

Why You Should Check Your Credit Report

Several studies show that a large percentage of adults seldom check their credit reports. It's imperative to check your credit report on a regular basis when you are the sole income earner.

Your credit report is used to make decisions about your financial future. This includes your ability to be approved for a credit card or loan, and it can influence your ability to rent a home or apartment, and of course, whether you can purchase a home, car, borrow money for college, or get hired for a job.

There are three major credit bureaus in the United States: Equifax, Experian, and TransUnion. Companies that you do business with have an agreement to forward your debt information to at least one of the three credit bureaus, usually on a monthly basis, which then updates that information in your credit report.

Various businesses, such as internet, cell phone, and utility companies, don't update your credit report with your monthly payments but will notify the credit bureaus if you default on your payments. When this occurs, these businesses might be listed on your credit report as debt collection. In addition, late payments can remain on your credit report for up to seven years.

How to Check Your Credit Report

You can check your credit report for free within a few minutes by going to www.annualcreditreport.com. You're entitled to one free copy of your credit report every year from each of the three reporting bureaus.

Once you have your credit report, review your personal information and all account information for accuracy. If you find errors, such as accounts you don't recognize, this could indicate fraudulent use of your credit. Check the credit bureau's website for its process to dispute an error. Correcting information on your report can usually be done online.

Why You Should Check Your Credit Report on a Regular Basis

Checking your credit report is smart, but contrary to what many financial experts recommend, once a year is not enough. After initially checking your credit reports with the three credit bureaus, you should consider spreading out requests for your free credit report to get one from each credit bureau every four months instead of getting them annually from all three credit bureaus at the same time. In addition, there are several free and easy-to-use apps that allow you to check your credit report more frequently, such as Credit Karma or CreditWise.

Why You Should Check Your Credit Score as Well

With all the security breaches and hacks in recent years, there's a chance that identity thieves have access to your personal information. Your credit score matters, and your credit score is a reflection of your credit report. The three digits that represent your credit score assist financial institutions in deciding whether to give you a loan and on what terms.

If your score is low, you may not get the best offers for insurance, cell phone plans, or other services where a credit check is required. In addition, you could be denied a loan to buy a car, purchase a house, or attend school. The higher your score, the less risky you appear to lenders.

How to Check Your Credit Score

There are dozens of credit score models, and credit scores can vary depending on what type of inquiry is being made (such as an auto lender versus a mortgage lender) and what credit bureau data are being used.

VantageScores are widely available for free online, and you can also get FICO scores for free from many financial institutions. Many lenders use VantageScores and FICO scores, and the two use a score range between 300 and 850. A score above 700 is generally considered good, while a score above 750 is considered to be very dependable.

When you request copies of your credit report or credit score, a credit request is being made on your behalf; this is called a soft inquiry. A soft inquiry is not used for making a lending decision like a hard inquiry, so it does not hurt your credit score.

Checking your credit score frequently will serve as a preventive measure from becoming a victim of identity fraud. If you notice a drop in your credit score, it is a good idea to review your credit report for any unusual activity.

VantageScores and FICO scores are both based on the same criteria:

- Your payment history
- How much you owe
- How long you've had credit
- Types of credit accounts you have open
- Recent inquires you have made to open new credit accounts

How to Raise Your Credit Score

- Pay all your bills on time. That affects 35 percent of your score.
- Don't carry a credit card balance or, at minimum, keep it below 30 percent of the limit.
- Responsibly manage a variety of debts, such as credit cards, a car loan, a mortgage, and student loans, while you are following the steps to live a life free of debt.
- Keep older credit card accounts, and avoid opening new ones.

How to Build Your Credit History

We live in a society where credit is necessary. For example, many employers scrutinize the credit history of job applicants, as do landlords when you're trying to rent an apartment. The length of your credit history can make it hard for young adults to have high credit scores. The reason why I was given a high interest rate of 13 percent when I purchased my first car in my early twenties was because I had not established a long-enough credit history.

Building a solid credit history while you're young can pay off over decades. Plus, one day when you buy a home, having a great credit score could save you tens of thousands of dollars in interest. That's because the best interest rates typically go to borrowers with the highest credit scores.

If you have little or no credit history, you'll need to build it. Opening a secured credit card may help. Secured cards are credit cards that are secured with a deposit. Some banks offer secured credit cards for customers who need to establish credit. Most often, cardholders must deposit between 100 percent and 200 percent of their desired credit limits. This deposit serves as collateral for the purchases you make using the card. If you default on your payments, the card issuer keeps your deposit. Otherwise, as long as you keep your account in good standing, your credit card issuer will return your deposit to you after a certain number of months or when you close the account. Getting a secured card, making a few purchases, and paying the bill off every month could help build your credit history.

List Your Debts

After you check your credit report, you will be able to make a list of all your creditors and the outstanding debt you owe to each of them. You can get the current balance for each debt by looking at the most recent billing statement. It's important that you stay current with all your creditors. If you are behind on any bills, it's time to get caught up and to start making the required minimum monthly payments.

How to Protect Yourself from Fraud

- **Credit freeze:** To protect yourself from identity fraud, you may want to freeze your credit. A credit freeze is a free tool that lets you restrict access to your credit report, which makes it more difficult for identity thieves to open new accounts in your name. In order to freeze your credit report, you will need to contact each of the three credit bureaus (Equifax, Experian, and TransUnion). You'll need to provide your name, address, date of birth, Social

Security number, and other identifying information. After receiving your free request, each credit bureau will provide you with a unique personal identification number (PIN) that you'll use if you choose to lift the freeze. A credit freeze remains in place until you ask the credit bureau to temporarily lift it or remove it altogether.

- **Identity theft protection:** Buying theft protection allows you to receive monitoring from all three credit bureaus, instead of just one, and it immediately alerts you whenever suspicious activity has been detected, such as someone using your identity to open a new cell phone account in your name. In addition, many identity theft services offer around-the-clock assistance with an expert who will walk you through the process if you become a victim of identity fraud. Finally, theft protection gives you the option to not only protect yourself but also your family members.

A copy of your credit report can provide insight into your financial habits to improve your credit score and can be used as a tool to assist you with getting out of debt.

CHAPTER 3

You Need an Emergency Savings Fund

f the 2018-2019 government shutdown didn't teach us anything else, it should be that all of us had better be saving for the unexpected.

As the sole income earner, you need an emergency savings fund more than anyone else does. The idea is to have enough money on hand so that you can stop depending on credit cards or payday or line-of-credit loans, or on drawing from your IRA or 401(k) account every time an unexpected expense comes up. When you have an emergency savings fund, you do not have to panic when the starter goes out on your car or when you have to take a few days off work because your child breaks his or her leg.

How Much You Should Have in Your Emergency Savings Fund

The old rule of thumb was to have $1,000 as the base level of money to start your emergency savings fund, and once your nonmortgage debt is paid off, you can then build your savings to three to six months of pay.

Having $1,000 in your emergency savings fund is better than having nothing, but unmarried people should consider saving more. With only one source of income coming in, there is less flexibility in the budget to withstand a financial emergency.

Based on my personal experience, I suggest you consider saving at least one to three months of living expenses as your base level to start your emergency savings fund, and once you have paid off your nonmortgage debt, building your emergency savings fund to nine to twelve months of living expenses.

That doesn't mean you have to stash that much cash at once. Your focus should be on what is within your reach and what you can put away every week or month to get closer to your savings goal. For example, putting $50 a week into a bank or credit union high-yield savings account would allow you to save $2,000 (before interest is earned) within ten months. If you are trying to pay down debt, switch to minimum payments for a while, and build up to this level of cash. A base level of one to three months of your living expenses in emergency savings covers the vast majority of the emergencies we face in life. Having this cushion could help lessen the chances that you'll turn to your credit card and add to debt you may be trying to pay off.

Once you pay down your nonmortgage debt, calculate an appropriate amount to determine your nine- to twelve-month savings goal. It's important to understand that this is not nine to twelve months of income, and it's not inclusive of all the money you spend in a typical, nonemergency month. Your emergency savings fund should have enough money so that you can pay your rent or mortgage, car payment, phone bill, utilities, and any other daily expenses during a crisis.

To calculate an appropriate amount, go through that budget you put together and decide on a line-by-line basis whether each expense is something that you would need to cover if you were faced with an unexpected life event. Once you have that amount, multiply it by a factor of nine to twelve. You now have your nine- to twelve-month emergency savings fund goal.

Nine to twelve months of savings will cover a real financial emergency you may face, including a job loss, major health crisis, or natural disaster, such as a hurricane.

If you have a stable job and a fairly nonstressful life with little volatility in your expenses, then nine months of savings is probably sufficient as long as that amount makes you comfortable. On the other hand, if you have dependent children or you're a high-income earner in a specialized occupation, you may need more savings because it may take you longer to find a new position in your field. At the end of the day, it's your judgment call to tailor the specific amount to your unique life circumstances.

Where You Should Put Your Emergency Savings

Do not invest your emergency savings into anything that might lose money. The place to keep your emergency savings fund is at a local bank or credit union in a money market or high-yield savings account that will provide immediate access if an emergency arises.

Many people are disappointed in the returns that a money market or savings account gives and want to put their money into investments, such as stocks, which can provide a higher potential for return. However, money market and savings accounts do not have the risk of losing money over time, and savings accounts are highly liquid, meaning you can withdraw the money whenever you need to without penalty.

How to Build an Emergency Savings Fund

- **Set up automatic savings.** Set up an automatic transfer of $25, $50, $100, or more from your checking account into your savings each payday.
- **Save unexpected income.** A tax refund, pay raise, bonus, cost-of-living adjustment, or extra income from a part-time job or side gig can contribute to growing a healthy savings. Directing at least part of this money to your emergency savings fund can help you reach your goal sooner.
- **Make minimum payments on your outstanding debt.** Paying off your debt is the ultimate goal but not until you have a base level of at least one to three months of living expenses on hand.
- **Negotiate your bills.** Call internet, cell phone, and other service providers and ask for a better rate. The best way to get a better rate is to research the lowest going rates in your area, either the price your provider is offering to new subscribers or rates offered by the competition, and use that price as leverage in your negotiation. When you call, ask to speak to the retention department, as this department usually has the authority to give you a better rate.
- **Start a coin jar.** Go through your wallet or purse, your home, your desk, and your car to locate all the spare change you can find. Put the change in a jar, and at the end of each month, deposit the change into your emergency savings fund. Doing this over time can create a robust savings account.
- **Pick up extra hours.** Let your coworkers know you are willing to pick up extra shifts in case they want to take some additional time off.
- **Refer friends and family.** You can receive credit toward bills you're already paying for referring new customers to service providers you use. Transfer the amount you would normally pay toward the bill into your emergency savings fund.

- **Negotiate your rent.** If you're a reliable tenant and you plan to continue living where you're currently renting, you may be able to request a longer-term lease in exchange for a lower monthly rental payment, which will be beneficial for you and your landlord.

How to Start a Side Gig

Finding time to make a little extra money on the side can be one of the fastest ways to build an emergency savings fund. Starting a side gig proves to be a viable option for many people who want to save money and are working to get out of debt.

A side gig is not a part-time job that entails someone else, such as an employer, calling the shots. A side gig gives you the flexibility to decide when you want to work and how much you want to earn, and it is completed outside of one's day job, usually during evenings, weekends, or vacation breaks.

You can start your own side gig that allows you to work from home, or you can complete work on a contract, on-call, or freelance basis for a company.

Although traditional part-time jobs are always an option, there are countless examples of side gigs. Some popular side gigs that many people engage in include the following:

- Teaching online courses
- Selling clothing
- Freelance editorial writer
- Personal home organizer
- Tutoring
- Coaching
- Survey taking
- Online juror
- Virtual office assistant
- Selling baked goods/catering
- Mystery shopping
- Modeling/acting
- Photographer/videographer
- Product demonstrator
- Direct sales
- Lawn services

- Maintenance services
- Housecleaning
- Housesitting
- Dog walking
- Pet sitting
- Digital designing
- Social media manager
- Blogger
- Website evaluator

All these ideas are great ways to earn extra income on the side, which can be beneficial in building your emergency savings fund and paying off your debt. Finally, the best way to take on a side gig is to establish your strengths and to determine what you enjoy and how much time you can invest.

In addition, when you have a side gig, your earnings may be taxable. You should speak to a certified financial accountant for tax advice.

When You Should Use Your Emergency Savings Fund

Once you have fully funded your emergency savings, you do not want to tap into the money unless you have an actual emergency that you couldn't foresee. For example, regular home maintenance should be a part of your monthly budget and not something you need to take from your emergency savings fund to pay for. And you know your car registration is due each year, so that's not a good use of these funds.

On the other hand, you can't plan for an emergency root canal or the time it may take to find a new job due to a layoff, so when you have a true emergency, tap into your account.

If you use your emergency fund, make it a priority to replenish it once you get back on your feet to protect yourself against subsequent emergencies.

Once I completed building my emergency savings fund, I felt a sense of peace and great accomplishment. I have needed it several times, and although spending unexpected money is never fun, it's great to know that you are financially prepared to face the unexpected stuff life will throw your way.

CHAPTER 4

Paying Off Your Debt Is Freeing

Now that you know the importance of creating a budget, checking your credit report and score, and building an emergency savings fund, let's discuss paying off your debt.

If you really want to have freedom in your life from the stress of monthly payments, then one of the most freeing things you can do as an unmarried person is to get out of debt.

Money doesn't solve all your problems, and no one should expect that living a life free of debt somehow brings instant happiness. However, I sleep a little better at night knowing that I owe no one. The feeling of security and comfort is well worth the effort of putting in the hard work and sacrifice.

The bottom line to paying off your debt is that you need to live on less than you make and to use the extra money to pay off your existing debts. If you need additional income, you should consider starting a side gig or getting a part-time job.

Debt Snowball or Debt Avalanche

There are several ways to pay off debt, but the methods I have used are the debt snowball and the debt avalanche.

Debt snowball is a debt-reduction strategy where you pay off debts in order of smallest to largest, gaining momentum as each balance is paid off. Using the debt snowball, you get a small win up front. Often you can pay off your smallest debt in a few months. Also, by the time you start focusing on the larger debts, such as your student loans or car balance, you have the confidence, ability, and cash flow to achieve your goal. The debt snowball uses the following steps:

1. Pay the minimum monthly payment on all your debts.
2. Devote any leftover money to the nonmortgage debt with the smallest balance.
3. Once that debt is paid off, devote its previous monthly payment and leftover money to your next smallest nonmortgage debt. After the second one is paid off, apply what you were paying on the first and second to pay off the third nonmortgage debt, and so forth.

Debt avalanche is similar to the debt snowball. The difference with the debt avalanche is that the order of your nonmortgage debt is not based on your balances but on their interest rates. You will pay less interest if you tackle the highest interest rate first. Saving money on interest means you will pay off your debts more quickly. The debt avalanche uses the following steps:

1. Make minimum monthly payments on all your debts.
2. Devote leftover money to nonmortgage debt with the highest interest rate.
3. Once that debt is paid off, devote its previous monthly payment and leftover money to the second-highest nonmortgage debt. Then work your way through to the lowest-interest-rate nonmortgage debt.

Create a list with the following columns:

- **Creditor:** The one to whom debt is owed.
- **Balance:** The amount of current debt.
- **Monthly payment:** The amount of monthly payment.
- **Rate:** The rate of interest charged for debt.
- **Priority:** Number the debts in the order you are going to pay them off.

Debt Snowball and Debt Avalanche Example				
Creditor	Balance	Monthly Payment	Rate	Snowball/Avalanche Priority
Credit card 1	$3,200	$70	10%	3/3
Credit card 2	$4,500	$102	15%	4/1
Store card	$250	$25	8%	1/4
Auto loan	$5,000	$480	3%	5/6
Mortgage	$135,000	$1,015	5%	
Bank loan	$1,000	$50	12%	2/2
Student loan	$15,000	$213	5%	6/5
TOTAL NONMORTGAGE DEBT = $28,950				
MINIMUM MONTHLY NONMORTGAGE DEBT PAYMENT = $940				

Using this example, let's say you are budgeting $1,000 a month to pay off debt. With your minimum monthly debt payment of $940, plus the leftover money in your budget of $60, using the debt snowball method, you would start applying the leftover money of $60 to the store card each month until you pay off the debt, which would take three months.

After paying off the store card, you would move up to the bank loan, which is the next smallest debt. You'd pay the monthly minimum of $50, plus the $25 (the previous monthly payment devoted to the store card) and the leftover money from your budget of $60, for a total monthly payment of $135. The bank loan would be paid off within seven months after paying off the store card debt. After paying off the bank loan, move up to the next smallest debt (credit card 1). You would pay off the student loan last.

Using the debt avalanche, you would start paying on credit card 2 first, and once you pay off that debt, you would move to the bank loan. Then the next debt in line becomes credit card 1.

If you create a payment plan of $1,000 each month and have total current non-mortgage debt of $28,950, then using the snowball method, you'd pay back with interest $31,366 and would be out of debt in 32 months. If you used the avalanche method, you would pay back with interest $31,105 and would be out of debt in 32 months. By using the avalanche method, you would save $261.

How to Choose the Method That's Best for You

If you need short-term victories to motivate you, then debt snowball is the method for you. If you are detailed and patient and want to target debts with the highest interest rates first, then debt avalanche should be your method of choice.

Knowing how much you could save can influence which method you use. You can use an online calculator or download an app that compares the debt snowball and debt avalanche methods to determine how long it will take to get out of debt and to see how much interest you will pay over time. Both methods will get you to the ultimate goal: living a life free of debt.

How to Build a Down Payment Car Fund

Once you pay off your current vehicle, the hope is that you'll continue to drive the same vehicle for several years if you keep up with the routine service and maintenance. However, at some point you will most likely need to purchase a new vehicle, and you want to be in a position to pay cash.

After paying off your nonmortgage debt, you should allocate the amount of the original car payment to set up a down payment car fund by putting money in a high-interest savings account so that it can grow. (All car-related expenses, including car payment, principle, interest, insurance, and other expenses, shouldn't exceed 10 percent of your pretax monthly income.) Using the previous example, the car payment was $480 per month, so after paying off your nonmortgage debt, you would deposit $480 in the down payment car fund each month. After 12 months you would have saved $5,760 (before interest is earned) toward the down payment of a new vehicle or for the purchase of a used vehicle. If you do this over 36 months, you would have $17,280, and after 60 months, you would have $28,800.

How to Pay Off Your Mortgage Debt

Once you've paid off your nonmortgage debt, you should contribute the leftover money to build your emergency savings fund with nine to twelve months of living expenses. Using the previous example, if you've been budgeting $1,000 to pay off your nonmortgage debt, and you put $480 toward the down payment car fund, you would have $520 left to put toward your emergency savings fund. After 12 months, you would have $6,240 (before interest is earned) in your emergency savings fund.

Within 36 months you would have $18,720, and after 60 months, you would have $31,200.

Once your emergency savings fund has nine to twelve months of living expenses, you should consider increasing contributions to your retirement savings account so that you're contributing the recommended 15 percent of your income to fully fund your account.

Next, ask your mortgage lender for an amortization schedule, and include an extra principal payment, along with your normal mortgage payment, so that you can start becoming mortgage-free before you retire.

Keep in mind that paying off your mortgage will not eliminate your homeowner association fees, real estate taxes, or homeowner's insurance. However, you will have the peace of mind, security, and pride that comes with really owning your home. And that's priceless.

How to Avoid Getting Back into Debt

To prevent yourself from going back into debt, you should consider the following:

1. **Decide that you want to remain debt-free.** It takes passion, energy, and focus to live a debt-free life. And it takes a lot of hard work and a firm commitment to incurring no additional debt.
2. **Learn to budget.** At the beginning of the month, either write down or use budgeting software to record your average income and expenses for the month, and do not allow yourself to spend any money that is not in the budget.
3. **If necessary, decrease your expenses and/or increase your income.** Before you had a budget, it may have been a challenge to know where your money went each month. Now that you have a budget, it might be apparent that you are spending too much on food or entertainment or that you need to increase your income by starting a side gig or part-time job.
4. **Stop using credit cards.** Paying with cash or using a debit card is essential to staying out of debt. However, if you must use credit cards, pay the balance off in full every month or within the billing grace period.
5. **Build up your emergency savings fund.** To remain debt-free, you should have some money set aside to cover the unexpected things life may throw at you.

Why You Should Celebrate Your Progress

Each time you pay off a debt, celebrate the fact that you'll never owe that debt again and that you have even more money to devote toward paying off the next debt.

Although I kept a monthly budget and tracked my spending, I made sure not to deprive myself. I believe, and am living proof, that you can get out of debt while still enjoying life. I continued to eat out, travel, and buy things I enjoyed. However, I only spent money I had. If I wanted or needed something and didn't have the cash on hand, I saved up for it first.

The first thing I experienced after getting out of debt was an unbelievable sense of freedom. It wasn't until my debt was gone that I fully realized just how much it had been weighing me down. Having this kind of peace of mind has been incredible.

So instead of getting discouraged about how far you still have to go, celebrate your progress along the way. Getting out of debt is very achievable, but be patient because it takes time.

CHAPTER 5

Invest in Your Future

Although I contributed to retirement savings, I didn't get serious with investing for retirement until I turned forty. As already discussed, I was a diligent saver and lived within my means in my thirties, but I put retirement savings on the back burner. However, this is the area that I wish I had contributed to more when I was in my twenties and thirties. As you learn over time in investing, compound interest can lead to a great amount of wealth down the line because you're gaining money from the interest you've already earned.

Planning for retirement is not a high priority for many people because it's easy to procrastinate when you feel you have time on your side and when you have other financial demands. However, starting with a budget, living within your means, and creating an income safety net by building your emergency savings fund puts you on the path to a successful financial future that eventually includes retirement. As an unmarried individual, you need special strategies for retirement savings, health care, and estate planning.

Where You Should Invest

Unmarried individuals need to take advantage of tax-deferred savings as early as possible because their income becomes subject to higher individual income tax rates more quickly than married couples. This can mean that unmarried individuals are losing more of their income to taxes, which results in less discretionary income and less ability to save. For most of us, the best place to invest will be in tax-deferred retirement savings accounts, such as a 401(k), 403(b), 457(b), IRA, or health savings account (HSA).

Roth 401(k) plans and Roth IRA accounts offer even more tax savings than tax-deferred accounts, so you'll pay taxes on your contributions now, but your earnings will grow tax-free, and you won't owe taxes when you withdraw the money for retirement, provided the five-year aging requirement has been satisfied, and you have met the 59½ age requirement.

Put a Percentage of Your Pay Raises into Retirement Savings

I do not recommend that you completely stop investing while paying off your debt. If you have an employer-sponsored savings plan that provides "free" matching funds, I suggest that you invest what it takes to take full advantage of any employer match, as long as you have the income to do so.

In addition, by increasing your savings over the years and decades by putting just 1 percent of your pay raises into retirement savings, along the way you should reach the recommended contribution target goal of saving 15 percent of your paycheck toward fully funding your retirement. This 15 percent goal includes any contributions you may get from your employer. For example, if your employer contributes 5 percent dollar for dollar in "free" matching funds, you would need to save 10 percent of your paycheck, which would get you to the recommended contribution goal of 15 percent.

The 15 percent target goal assumes that a person retires at age 67, which is when most people will be eligible for full Social Security benefits. If you don't plan to work until that long, you will most likely need to save more than 15 percent of your paycheck. If you plan to work longer, your required savings rate could be lower.

Catch-Up Contributions

If you're fifty or older, be sure to make the most of catch-up contributions to your retirement savings plan after paying off your nonmortgage debt and building your emergency savings fund. This option enables savers to increase contributions at a time when retirement draws near. Age fifty catch-up contributions are possible in employer-sponsored 401(k), 403(b), and 457 plans. Also, you can contribute to an IRA. Go to your retirement plan administrator or www.irs.gov to learn more about annual catch-up contribution limits.

Every person's circumstances are different, so you should do some research through reputable online sites or meet with a certified financial planner, preferably a fiduciary financial adviser, who can assist you with developing your own plan based on your age, risk tolerance, goals, time frame, and other personal factors. (Only fiduciary financial advisers are legally and ethically required by law to recommend investments in the client's best interests, not their own, when managing and advising clients about investing.)

Understand Social Security

Unmarried individuals have fewer options than their married friends, especially those who have never been married, because their Social Security benefits are based solely on their work histories. If you were married for a decade or more and then divorced, or your spouse passed away, you may qualify for Social Security benefits based on his or her work history.

Pre-retirees who fail to plan could be leaving serious Social Security money on the table. You can retire at any time between age 62 and full retirement age. For example, if you were born between 1955 and 1959, your full retirement age is 66, and if you were born after 1960, your full retirement age is 67. If you start benefits early, your benefits are reduced a fraction of a percent for each month before your full retirement age. If you are in good health, each year you wait past full retirement age—up to age 70— you could get an increase in your benefit.

The Social Security Administration stopped mailing paper statements to workers who are under age sixty, so if you do not have a "My Social Security" account online, you should open one now. You can sign up online at www.ssa.gov/myaccount.

Having an account and checking it annually will give insight into the earnings you've paid Social Security tax on. Your employer reports those earnings to the government through a W-2. Even if retirement is decades away, and even if you are skeptical that you'll get the Social Security benefits you've been promised, it is important to check your account for accuracy.

Your Social Security statement contains two important pieces of information.

- First, it has your earnings history. This is important because your Social Security benefit is calculated based on your thirty-five highest-earning years of work. You want to be sure it's correct.

- Second, your statement will give you a projection of what to expect when you do eventually file for benefits.

If you have a credit freeze, you may experience difficulty signing up for "My Social Security." I know because I ran into trouble setting up my account. To expedite the sign-up process, visit a local Social Security office, and make sure you carry multiple forms of identification to prove your identity. There, a local agent will be able to give you a special activation code that will allow you to complete the registration online.

Medicare

Most people age sixty-five or older are eligible for free Medicare Part A (hospital care) if they have worked and paid Medicare taxes long enough. You should sign up for Medicare Part A (hospital care) three months before your sixty-fifth birthday, whether or not you want to begin receiving retirement benefits. If you wait longer, your Medicare Parts B (medical coverage) and D (prescription drug coverage) may cost you more money in late enrollment penalties.

If you have an HSA or your medical insurance coverage is under a group health plan based on your employment, you may want to contact your insurance company or human resources department to find out how signing up for Medicare will affect you. To learn more about Medicare, go to www.medicare.gov.

Long-Term Care

You may want to consider investing in Long-Term Care Insurance (LTCI) because Medicare and traditional healthcare usally do not cover the basic cost of support and services associated with long term custodial and personal care needs due to aging, prolonged disease, illness, or injury. LTCI is designed to cover assistance with the activities of daily living that people are unable to perform such as walking, dressing, bathing, eating, toileting, continence, and getting in and out of a chair or bed; be it in your home, or in a nursing or assisted living community. Speak to a licensed broker who can assist you in looking at the available options.

Estate Planning

As an unmarried individual, if you pass away without a will, the laws of the state will prevail, which means relatives you barely knew (or didn't get along with) could inherit your assets.

If you do not have children, it typically starts with surviving parents, then siblings, nearest relatives, and so on, with the entirety of the assets going to the first one living on the list. Instead of letting the state decide, it's best to draw up a will and other estate documents.

Before drafting your estate documents, you'll want to decide who will oversee your health-care and end-of-life decisions if you become incapacitated and who will serve as the executor of your will. This can be tricky for unmarried individuals. But getting the right documents in place will make things easier if age or illness leaves you unable to manage your own affairs or make medical decisions, and it could prevent ugly court battles among your heirs after you're gone.

Most unmarried individuals find family and friends to carry out their wishes. Consider naming a successor (alternate person) in case the first person you've chosen isn't available. Also, your executor should know where your important papers are kept and be given a key in case he or she has to enter your home.

There are online resources available to complete your estate documents; however, I suggest you hire a dedicated estate-planning attorney to fully understand the various options you have for planning and to make sure your forms comply with state laws. These are the legal documents you'll need:

- **Durable power of attorney:** This gives someone you select the power to represent you and to manage your health, legal, and financial matters if you become incapacitated.
- **Advance directive, or living will:** This spells out your wishes regarding what specific actions should be taken for your health if you are no longer able to make decisions for yourself because of illness or incapacity.
- **Last will and testament:** These name one or more persons as executors, who will oversee the distribution of your estate and make sure your taxes, debts, and other obligations are paid upon your passing.
- **Revocable trust:** If you're providing support for an aging parent or family member and don't want it interrupted by months of probate to carry out the terms of a will, then you may want to consider a trust based on your most important estate goals and objectives.

When estate planning, unmarried individuals with minor children should also consider who will get custody of their children if something were to happen to them. This is most commonly called a *guardian*. The individuals named as guardians will take legal guardianship of minor children. In addition, any assets going to the children as beneficiaries should go into a testamentary trust controlled by a trustee you designate.

One of the greatest gifts you can leave your loved ones is an organized estate. Do not delay in preparing your will.

Continue Maintaining Social Connections

For many people, work is their source of contact with people; however, that source goes away with retirement. Growing older without a significant other or adult children means you'll need to build lasting relationships with extended family and trusted friends. To prevent yourself from becoming increasingly isolated, you should expand your social network before retirement by incorporating some of the following activities into your lifestyle:

- **Volunteer.** Get involved with civic or faith-based activities.
- **Stay current.** Keep up with trends and new ways of doing things through new forms of technology.
- **Start a side gig.** Many retirees continue to supplement their retirement income with a side gig or part-time job.
- **Stay physically healthy.** Make exercise fun by joining a gym and participating in fitness classes.
- **Continue education.** Many community colleges offer free or discounted courses to senior students in culinary arts, foreign language, gardening, painting, or other active areas of study.
- **Join a senior dating site.** A dating site can be a great way to meet others online before committing to meeting them in real life.
- **Look at online senior meet-up groups.** These online sites connect individuals with others with common interests and skills versus those interested in dating.

Get the most out of retirement by being financially ready, staying healthy, and enjoying time with others. There is no reason you shouldn't be out and about and having fun during this season of your life.

CHAPTER 6

Things to Consider before Buying a Home

made the decision to purchase my first home after receiving a letter from my property manager stating that my rent would increase by $300 if I chose to renew my lease. I felt I would be better off owning a home instead of renting, so I made an appointment with a mortgage lender who determined based on my income and credit score how much of a loan I would qualify for. The mortgage lender referred me to a Realtor, whom I immediately started working with. After a day or so of looking at homes, I found a "cute" home in a nice community, and within thirty days of finding the home, I closed on it. What I failed to do prior to purchasing my first home was to research the area and to project all the unexpected costs of owning a new home.

Within thirty months of purchasing my new home in the Hickory Hill area of Memphis, Tennessee, the community went through a demographic change after being annexed by the City of Memphis. Major stores and businesses pulled out of the area, which resulted in lower home property values. In addition, a large percentage of homeowners sold or rented their homes. The once-upscale area of Memphis became a community of blight where a high number of homeowners stopped maintaining their properties.

My neighborhood remained one of the nicer communities up until the Great Recession, which contributed to plummeting home values as a result of homeowners going into foreclosure. Although I was never in jeopardy of losing my home, I certainly lost thousands of dollars when I sold my home due to its lower market value. I learned as a homeowner that you shouldn't buy a home because it's "cute," and investing in a home is not a surefire way to build wealth. The bottom line is that you can be wise with your money, but the actions of others can cause you to lose tens of thousands of dollars on your investment.

Buying a home is the largest investment most people make in their lives. Conventional wisdom says that buying a home is a smarter financial decision than renting. However, homeownership can be an expensive option, especially for unmarried people. Owning a home is not for everyone, and for some, renting can be the more cost-effective option.

Contemplate the following if you're not buying a home with 100 percent cash:

- If you might move in the next five years, it may be best to rent because it usually takes five or more years for your investment in a home to make money. You should stay in the home long enough for the equity you get from paying the mortgage to outweigh the cost of selling your home, such as Realtor commissions, transfer and capital gains taxes, and escrow fees.
- You can most likely buy a home with a low credit score, but you should have a FICO score of 740 or higher because you'll typically qualify for the lowest interest rate with a high credit score. For example, the difference between a 620 credit score and a 740 score could add a full 1 percent to the rate you will pay for your loan, which will result in you paying tens of thousands of dollars extra over the life of the loan.
- Pay down your credit card balances and debt. Reducing your debt will help you qualify for the best possible mortgage terms.
- Have cash on hand in your emergency savings account. Lenders want to know that if you get sick or lose your job, you can cover the mortgage for a few months.
- You should put at least 10 percent down. A 20 percent down payment is even better. The money used for the down payment should not come from your emergency savings fund.
- You will most likely be required to pay mortgage insurance if you can't afford a 20 percent down payment. Mortgage insurance lowers the risk to the lender of making a loan to you so that you can qualify for a loan that you might not otherwise be able to get. In other words, mortgage insurance protects the lender's interests (not yours), and it increases the cost of your loan. If you are required to pay mortgage insurance, it will most likely be included in your total monthly payment that you make to your lender. In addition, depending

on the type of loan, you may be required to pay an up-front fee as part of your closing costs. And because the majority of your mortgage payments are going toward interest, you're not building a lot of equity when you have to pay mortgage insurance.

- Determine how much monthly take-home (after-tax) income you bring in by looking at your budget.

- Housing is generally the greatest monthly expense; therefore, you should aim to keep your mortgage payment at or below 25 percent of your monthly take-home income. This will leave room in your budget to achieve other goals and gives you greater leeway should you experience a medical problem, job loss, or another emergency. Therefore, if your take-home income is $5,000 a month, then your mortgage should be $5,000 x 0.25, or no more than $1,250 per month. Don't forget to add property taxes and homeowner's insurance as well as homeowner association fees and mortgage insurance (if applicable). It's important to keep in mind that when you're approved for a mortgage, lenders will likely approve you for a loan amount with payments of up to 35 percent of your pretax income. That may tempt you to take on more home than you should, but there's a big difference between pretax and after-tax income. Don't assume that just because the lender approved it, you can afford it. Remember, the more you spend on a home, the less money you have for everything else.

- Most homeowners choose a thirty-year fixed mortgage. The interest over that length of time will cause you to pay significantly beyond the original price. If possible, seek a fifteen-year mortgage. Your monthly payment will be higher, but you'll pay off your mortgage in half the time and you could save tens of thousands of dollars off the duration and amount of the loan.

- Research whether the local government has passed any bills or measures, such as annexing an unincorporated area into the community, where you plan to buy. Consider the pros and cons of annexation and how it could affect the future value of the home you're buying.

Understand All the Unexpected Costs of Buying a Home

- **Moving expenses:** You may want to ask for assistance from family and friends to help move your personal belongings if you are moving a short distance.

However, if you are moving to another city or state and have a lot of stuff, you may need to hire movers, which can cost you tens of thousands of dollars based on the distance they need to travel to deliver it.

- **Installing new locks:** Changing the locks on your new home and getting new keys should be an essential part of your move-in process. If you're handy, it will cost you very little to change the locks yourself. However, if you hire a qualified professional locksmith, it could cost you anywhere from $100 to $500, which varies in total cost by lock type, fees, and security level.

- **Furniture and décor:** Turning your house into a home can cost upward of tens of thousands of dollars when you add painting, furnishings, bedding, accent pieces, and window treatments to all the rooms.

- **Utilities:** This can be a big increase if you previously lived in an apartment where your utilities, such as water and trash, were included in the rent. Ask the seller if you can see a copy of a recent utility bill so that you can get an idea of a monthly average for gas, electricity, and water.

- **Ongoing maintenance and repairs:** Landscaping, carpet cleaning, pressure washing, pest and termite control, roofing and siding repairs, gutter cleaning, HVAC inspections and upkeep, and hiring a professional to remove animals, such as squirrels and raccoons, from your attic during the winter months are just a few costs you need to be aware of.

- **Homeowner association (HOA):** This is an organization in a subdivision, planned community, or condominium that makes and enforces rules for the properties within a jurisdiction. Those who purchase property within an HOA automatically become members and are required to pay either monthly or annual HOA fees for the upkeep of common areas and the building.

- **Property taxes:** This can be the second-largest expense of owning a home, after mortgage interest. In most areas, property taxes are governed by state law but are assessed and collected by the county based on the value of the home. Property taxes are calculated annually by applying a certain tax rate, and homeowners continue to pay property taxes on an annual basis.

- **Homeowner's insurance:** Protecting your home from damage comes at a much larger price than renting, and depending on where you live, home-owner's insurance ranges from $600 to upward of $2,100 annually, with a deductible of $500 to $1,000 or more. Renters insurance, meanwhile, is usu-ally less than $25 per month.

These extra costs could add an additional 30 percent to your base mortgage amount. If the mortgage is $1,250 a month, your total housing cost might be around $1,625. The decisions you make on your mortgage will have financial ramifications for years to come. Consider all the unexpected costs to make sure you can truly afford buying a home.

Don't Be the Prey for the Predator

Predatory lending is any lending practice that imposes unfair or abusive loan terms on a borrower. The predatory lending cycle continues to repeat itself in the area of home mortgages. Because home loans are backed by a borrower's real property, a predatory lender can profit not only from loan terms but also from the sale of a foreclosed home if a borrower defaults.

When buying a home, you will either pay on the front end by putting down an adequate down payment, or you will pay on the back end with a higher monthly mortgage payment and tens of thousands of dollars in extra interest payments, which could ultimately lead to unmanageable debt, ruined credit, foreclosure, or even the possibility of becoming homeless. There are several lending options available, especially for first-time home buyers, but don't allow yourself to get caught up in the zero-down, low-credit options when buying a home.

Buying a home is a very personal decision, and it's a huge financial and emotional commitment. Although many say that homeownership is essential for financial security, it's not the only option available to you. Depending on your circumstances, renting can give you more discretionary income each month and more freedom to pursue your other financial goals, such as paying off student loan debt or fully funding your retirement.

However, there are a lot of benefits to owning a home, such as pride of ownership, more predictable expenses, and more stability than renting because costs are usually based on a fixed-rate mortgage, and the ability to control things about your living situation that you can't control as a renter, such as decorating and renovations. You should use an online calculator or download an app to compare the cost of buying versus renting.

Ask for and check references before you select a lender or real estate agent who can assist you in figuring out how much you can afford and what kind of home you can expect to find based on the price range in the market where you want to buy.

CHAPTER 7

You Need Disability Insurance

I n addition to having auto, health, and renters or homeowner's insurance, there are several reasons why an unmarried person needs disability insurance. Think for a moment about what would happen if you were injured or ill and couldn't work. Would your emergency savings be enough to live on until Social Security benefits go into effect? If not, then you need it.

It's estimated that one in four Americans will become disabled for some period of time before retirement. Experts say disability insurance is critical for everyone who depends on income from a job. Most disabilities are caused by chronic medical conditions, such as the following:

- Arthritis
- Back pain
- Broken bones
- Cancer
- Carpal tunnel syndrome
- Complications during pregnancy or giving birth
- Depression, stress, or anxiety
- Diabetes
- Heart disease
- Herniated disk
- Runner's knee

- Rehab
- Surgery recovery
- Tennis elbow
- Whiplash

In other words, just about anyone at anytime could become disabled for a period of time.

How to Get Disability Insurance

Try to enroll in association or group plans because they're easier to qualify for. Many employers provide or offer disability insurance to their employees. Getting group insurance is easy; all you have to do is opt in during open enrollment. Most workplace plans generally include two policies:

- **Short-term disability insurance (STDI):** This usually covers 60 to 70 percent of your salary for 30 to 120 days, with a maximum benefit period of 52 weeks, if you miss work due to a nonwork-related illness or injury. Although the time period for which the coverage extends differs among companies and employers, short-term coverage typically lasts between 3 and 6 months. Coverage usually kicks in between 1 to 14 days after the diagnosis or injury, and there are sometimes caps on the monthly payment amount.
- **Long-term disability insurance (LTD):** This usually pays 50 to 67 percent of your salary for an extended time that may last until you are age 65.

Most employer policies are calculated on base salary only, without commissions or bonuses, and the payments may be taxable. However, most group plans are more affordable than buying your own policy independently. This can be a benefit when it's hard to find the room in your budget for extra premiums.

Private Disability Insurance

If you do not have group or association plans available to you, then you may want to consider purchasing private disability insurance. If you're looking to buy your own coverage, forget about short-term policies. You're better off putting the money into emergency savings.

However, you would benefit from buying your own long-term coverage because you can keep it if you leave your job and you avoid paying a higher premium to start a new policy at an older age.

Expect long-term disability insurance to cost around 1 to 3 percent of your salary. All LTD policies require that a claimant remain disabled for a period of time between when the disability begins and the receipt of your first check. Most commonly, these periods are 30, 60, or 90 days or longer. The longer elimination period, the lower the premiums. Just remember, you'll have to use your emergency savings until coverage kicks in. Most experts typically recommend a 90-day elimination period.

Insurance companies that sell private disability policies provide benefit periods as short as 2 years and as long as right up to retirement age of 67 when Social Security benefits would take over. A benefit period to age 67 is typically recommended. In addition, have a benefit of at least 60 to 65 percent of your income because benefits are tax-free if you ever make a claim.

Disability insurance gives you peace of mind while allowing you to continue paying your bills and providing for yourself and those you care for while you're out of work for an extended period of time. Consult with an independent insurance broker to learn what coverage options are right for you.

COBRA

It's important to be familiar with your employer's group health plan, especially when you're on short- or long-term disability. COBRA generally requires that group health plans sponsored by employers offer employees and their families the opportunity for temporary extension of health coverage under certain instances, where coverage under the plan would otherwise end, and it offers employees the opportunity to pay the entire premium for coverage up to 102 percent of the cost of the plan.

One of the worst things that could happen while on short-term or long-term disability is letting your health-care insurance lapse, so be proactive during your employer's benefits open enrollment and take note of the cost of COBRA and when the continuation of benefits under COBRA begin. Having 9 to 12 months or more in emergency savings is important because COBRA can run upward of $500 to $1,000 or more per month while you're on short-term or long-term disability.

CHAPTER 8

You Also Need Life Insurance

Many people feel that life insurance is for married couples or for unmarried people with dependents, but unmarried people without dependents also need to insure themselves. Here's why adding coverage is important.

- **Pay funeral costs:** No one likes to think about such things, but without some kind of life insurance, parents, other relatives, or loved ones will end up paying the funeral costs if you die unexpectedly. There can be other end-of-life expenses, too, such as hospital bills or other costs associated with your home, work, or personal life.
- **Pay debt:** Many people make the assumption that debt dies with them, but that's not always guaranteed. Personal loans that have a cosigner are generally not forgiven. For example, if you jointly owned a house, or if someone cosigned for a private student loan through a bank or other financial institution, in both instances the individuals who cosigned would still be responsible for paying the rest of the loan. Cosigned student loans issued through the federal government are forgiven.
- **Leave a legacy:** Life insurance can ensure that the important people in your life, such as aging parents you may care for and support or someone else who depends on you financially, are taken care of if something happens to you. Furthermore, you can leave a legacy by making a donation to a favorite charity or cause in your name.

- **Get the best rates:** Purchasing life insurance when you are young and healthy may allow you to lock in lower rates. That's because, as you get older, the rates usually increase. If you plan to get married and have children one day, buying life insurance when you are young can protect your future insurability because insurance companies often let clients add coverage at a later date without having to go through new underwriting.

For just a few dollars a month, you can make sure that should the worst happen to you, your family members will be provided for. Even if you're in your fifties or sixties and in good health, you can still find a life insurance plan that will cover your final expenses at a decent rate.

There are several types of affordable coverage available to fit your needs and budget. Many life insurance companies offer helpful product information on their websites, along with free quotes. It's smart to shop around to see which coverage is right for you, and it's recommended that you select coverage with companies rated A or better. If you still have questions, then a qualified life insurance professional can recommend which life insurance options are best for you.

CHAPTER 9

Make an Impact

Happiness comes from service, and God designed each of us to serve through our giving. God knows we're at our best when we give. Some people think that they can enjoy giving only when they have a lot of money or a successful career. But that's not true. Giving is one of the best investments you can make toward achieving genuine happiness. True giving comes from the heart, with no expectation of reciprocation. However, what we make happen for others, God will always make happen for us.

While you're becoming debt-free, you can still make an impact. Here are a few ways you can serve by giving.

Give Tithes

Even though I grew up in church and saw my parents make an impact by giving and serving through volunteerism, in my twenties I found myself staying focused only on my own needs. However, God continued to put people in my life who emphasized the importance of giving. Over time I began walking in faith and started to give through tithing.

The giving of our money is an act of worship and trust in God. For those not familiar with tithing, it is the practice of giving 10 percent of your income to your church. When we are able to give 10 percent of our income instead of keeping that money for ourselves, it shows that our heart isn't tied to our money and that we love God more than our money. The money is used to pay for a variety of services, such as heating and electricity, and other basic expenses used to run the church. Tithes also benefit special programs, such as international missions and local charities, and are also used to purchase food and other supplies for the less fortunate members of the community. This, of course, depends on how many members the church has and how much money is given to the church.

When I first began tithing, I found it to be difficult because I was working very hard for every dollar I made. However, over time I became more grateful to be able to give. I have sacrificed some things along the way, but I am glad that I stopped making excuses by thinking I would start to tithe when I made more money or received a pay raise. I realized if I wasn't open to tithing $100 when I made $1,000, I definitely would not be tithing $1,000 when I made $10,000. I have made it a habit to make tithing my most important item when making my monthly budget. If you do not belong to a church, you can still give a percentage of your income to charities and to the causes that matter most to you.

Give to Charity

Giving to charity is very gratifying because you are donating to the causes you care about and believe in. You may donate money or property (such as clothing and household items), and donating to a charity can inspire your loved ones to do the same.

- **Run, walk, or bicycle for a good cause.** Numerous charity runs, walks, or bicycle rides are held each year. Sign up and participate in raising funds for a good cause.
- **Sponsor a child.** There's always the opportunity to sponsor underprivileged children from our country and from countries around the world.
- **Donate food.** Make a food or monetary donation to your local food bank. Many need all the food and money they can get to be able to serve those in need.
- **Shop at the right places.** Many businesses donate part of their proceeds to charities. Check with the merchants you shop at regularly to see if they offer opportunities to donate to organizations as part of your purchase.
- **Give blood.** Donating blood to your local blood bank is free and doesn't take much time. More importantly, your donation could help save someone's life.
- **Donate after natural disasters.** When natural disasters strike, they bring out the best impulses in many of us. We feel empathy for the victims and an urge to reach out and help them in any way we can. Due to the logistical challenges associated with such tangible goods as food, clothes, and toiletries,

after most natural disasters it's best to give cash (first), time and labor (second), and goods and services (third).

Before you donate money or goods, research the charity. Be certain that the charity is real and adheres to 501(c)(3) requirements. Several agencies, such as the IRS, your state's attorney general's office, and the Better Business Bureau, offer tips, databases, and reports that help you evaluate the operation of charities.

Give Back to Your Community

Volunteering is certain to bring good results for everyone involved. There are countless ways to serve in your community. Those who receive help are grateful for it, and volunteers learn that helping others makes them feel better.

- **Share your talents.** Each of us has been given talents from God that we should develop and use to serve others. Examine your life and see what talents you have and what you are good at. If you are good at computers, building, gardening, organizing, cooking, or working with your hands, then you should use your talents to assist those in need.
- **Serve children and teenagers.** So many children and teenagers need our help, and we can give it. There are many programs to become involved with helping children, and you can easily become a mentor. Children need role models and people who care about their lives and behavior. Whether you read stories to children at a local school or coach a youth league, your efforts will be appreciated. Moreover, you can make an investment that will pay dividends in the future.
- **Serve with senior citizens.** Many opportunities exist to serve older adults. Many seniors simply need the connection that comes from relationships; others benefit from support services, including meal delivery and transportation. Service to seniors not only benefits older adults but also the people who share their stories, experiences, and friendship.
- **Volunteer to help veterans.** Serve those who have served our country. With such issues as homelessness, PTSD, disability, and unemployment facing our nation's veterans, they need all the help they can get. Whether grocery shopping or running errands, doing yard work or painting a veteran's home, there's a need you can help fulfill in your community.

- **Volunteer at a hospital.** Hospital volunteers create the ideal patient and family experiences for all hospital visitors. Volunteer opportunities include everything from giving support in the gift shops and admissions department to being a patient visitor escort to manning information booths to sitting with patients or working with children. Hospitals have a wide variety of volunteer needs that are suitable for all ages.
- **Visit animal shelters.** They will be glad you're willing to spend some time with their animals. Dogs and cats need to be loved daily.

Pray for Someone in Need

Praying is incredibly powerful. The power of prayer should never be underestimated because it draws on the glory and might of the powerful God of the universe. You may not have the money to help someone, but you cannot lose much by including someone in your prayers. Send them some love and wish them strength, peace, and comfort to see things through.

Exercise Your Right to Vote

In addition to serving through giving, you can make an impact by voting. As an unmarried person, almost every single aspect of your life, such as issues on health care, pay equality, college affordability, women's rights, and workers' rights, is affected by politics, and every single decision is made by politicians who were put into office by those who voted.

Your vote matters not only in the presidential election but also for elected local and state politicians who pass laws that directly affect your day-to-day life. So stay informed and exercise your right to vote.

If you're still not sure you have the money, time, or energy to serve through giving, then consider this: many studies have shown that giving can protect your health and prolong your life. Recognize that others helped you achieve your merits, and now you have the opportunity to make an impact by paying it forward. You don't have to be rich, powerful, or influential to effect change, and we all have the gift of giving; we just have to activate it. I believe each of us can make quite an impact on this world.

CHAPTER 10

Before You Wed

Contentment doesn't mean you can't have ambition. It means enjoying where you are on your way to where you're going. Although I'm content with being single and do not consider marriage necessary to complete my life, I am open to marrying a wonderful man. I have learned through the years to look to God as my provider and to be patient, faithful, and productive during this season of my life.

No one owes anyone an explanation for being single; however, I'm in contact with many unmarried people, and I've found there are basically three types of people living the single life.

- **Content and satisfied:** Some of these individuals are single at heart, and living single is how they live their most meaningful lives. Others are divorced or have never been married, but they have been in relationships that left them doubtful of the union of marriage.
- **Content but open to marrying:** These are individuals, such as myself, who are open to marrying but who have chosen not to marry just for the sake of marrying. Contrary to what society may think, this doesn't make us picky or mean we're looking for perfection; it makes us wise in knowing that we are looking for someone with whom we will be compatible and who shares the same values and has similar goals and interests. Most important, we are looking for someone with whom to have a true connection.
- **Seeking:** These individuals want to be married. Most often they're not pressed or desperately looking for someone to marry, but they just are not the single type.

When talking to unmarried individuals, in particular those who are *seeking*, the conversation usually turns to dating and marriage. It doesn't matter if I'm talking to people in their twenties, forties, sixties, or older; I have found that they're dating or looking to date someone who has a steady job, makes a good income, shares the same faith, and is educated, trustworthy, successful, and fun—the qualities go on and on. One thing I seldom hear is that they're dating or looking for someone to date and possibly marry who knows how to manage money. Considering that many studies show that money is the number one thing married couples argue about, as well as one of the top reasons why they divorce, I hope that finding a person who knows how to manage money is of great importance.

Communication Is Essential

Unfortunately, most people decide to get married without discussing their debt from student loans, car loans, credit cards, and shopping and gambling habits. Money can become a bigger issue if one partner is responsible with money and the other partner does not know how to manage money, or if one person in the relationship is overly conservative with money and the other one enjoys spending money on designer brands, entertainment, and travel. Even if one person in the relationship has perfect credit, banks will take the lower of the two credit scores.

Although every relationship is different, first and foremost, I pray that God is at the center of your relationship, and I hope you and your partner make it a goal to have open communication, which is one of the most important aspects of a satisfying marriage.

In order to prevent conflict in your marriage, it's especially important to have an open discussion (preferably before the proposal), about your finances and to understand each other's values and goals in regard to money. For example, both of you may be debt-free, but one person in the relationship may believe in tithing while the other is not open to it, or one person may be wealthy and believes in a prenuptial agreement while the other person is totally against entering into a marriage contract. What if one person has children, and he or she decides to list the children as primary beneficiaries on the life insurance policy instead adding the new spouse as the primary beneficiary?

Without open communication and a solid financial plan for how you'll handle money, you will have disagreements about it. You can save yourselves years of stress by discussing your values and goals about money prior to getting married. In addition, you should review each other's credit reports from each of the three credit bureaus

(Equifax, Experian, and TransUnion) so that the two of you establish the amount of debt you're bringing into the marriage.

You and your partner may want to go through in-depth premarital counseling with a minister or marriage counselor during your engagement to make sure you're both on the same page so that you know what you're getting yourself into should you choose to get married.

LET'S REFLECT

Whether you've worked your way through this book by reading page by page or you skipped around looking for the chapters that are most important to you, I hope this book has inspired, encouraged, and uplifted you to live a debt-free life.

My life is an example that living debt-free is an ongoing journey. It won't always be easy, but it will be fulfilling. When you reach this point, you will not be so stressed out when you experience a life event. When your finances are in order, your approach and attitude toward life will make a big difference in your mood, health, and relationships with others.

Taking responsibility for what's happening in your life is one of the most empowering things you can do. To succeed, you must stay focused on what's important and pursue your goals without wavering or hesitating. It can be intimidating to take charge of your finances, but you'll be amazed at the joy and freedom it brings. Beginning is usually the hard part. The journey starts with a single step; after that it gets easier. But look out: Old attitudes and habits will try to resurface and come back stronger than ever. Don't let them. The road to success is an uphill climb. So be patient. It will take time to get there, but anything worthwhile is worth working for. Will you make mistakes along the way? Of course. But there's nothing like the feeling of living a life free of debt. God's plan for each of us is to be an instrument to fulfill his will, and that can surely be achieved when we take control of our finances. Keep your eyes on the finish line, and trust God to help you. Stay faithful!

I love to hear from my readers and I invite you to send me a message and join my mailing list at www.liviakellyauthor.com.

ACKNOWLEDGMENTS

Having an idea and turning it into my first book is as hard as it sounds and more rewarding than I could have ever imagined. Appreciation is expressed to the following people who directly and indirectly contributed in small and great ways to my success in completing this book:

First and foremost, I would like to thank God for his never-ending grace, mercy, and provision because without him none of this would be possible.

To my mother and late father, without whom I would never have enjoyed so many opportunities, I thank you for encouraging me to follow my dreams and for teaching me that failure is not about losing; it's about not trying.

To my family and friends, thank you for your prayers, wisdom, and continual sources of unending inspiration.

To *everyone* who ever taught, coached, mentored, or preached something to me, thank you!

And a special thanks to the following: Jenny Chandler and her team at Elite Authors, who provided editing, cover design, and marketing; Crystal Green and her team at UIM (Uniquely Inspired Moments), who assisted with website development and social media branding; Rhonda Minor, who assisted with initial editing; Kathy Averhart, professional hair artist and owner of Definition of Hair, and Suzanne Mohr, Makeup Artist (Beauty Marked Midtown), who both assisted with my author photo look; Nicole Tyler and her team at Nicole Tyler Photography, who shot my author photo; TJ McBride Ministries, for always encouraging me to walk in faith and not by sight; and Washington State Hall of Fame Track and Field Coach Mike Hanby, my high school track coach, who over the years has stayed in contact with me and was the first to teach me the importance of writing and visualizing my goals. Thanks to ALL of you for keeping me focused and on track.

ENDNOTES

1. "America's Families and Living Arrangements: 2016, Table A1." United States Census Bureau. Accessed August 14, 2017. www.census.gov/data/tables/2016/demo/families/cps-2016.html.

2. "Table HH-4. Households by Size: 1960 to Present." United States Census Bureau. Accessed August 14, 2017. www.census.gov/population/socdemo/hh-fam/tabHH-4.pdf.

3. "The Share of Americans Living Without a Partner Has Increased, Especially among Young Adults." Richard Fry. Pew Research Center. October 11, 2017. www.pewresearch.org/fact-tank/2017/10/11/the-share-of-americans-living-without-a-partner-has-increased-especially-among-young-adults.

4. "About One-Third of US Children Are Living with an Unmarried Parent." Gretchen Livingston. Pew Research Center. April 27, 2018. www.pewresearch.org/fact-tank/2018/04/27/about-one-third-of-u-s-children-are-living-with-an-unmarried-parent.

5. "Benefits Planner | Life Expectancy." Social Security Administration. Accessed January 25, 2019. www.ssa.gov/planners/lifeexpectancy.html.

6. "Understanding Women's Financial Needs and Behavior." AARP. January 2007. www.aarp.org/money/investing/info-2007/women_finances.html.

7. "The Share of Americans Living Without a Partner Has Increased, Especially among Young Adults." Richard Fry.

Financial Resources

- AARP: www.aarp.org
- AnnualCreditReport.com: www.annualcreditreport.com
- Consumer Financial Protection Bureau (CFPB): www.consumerfinance.gov
- Debt.org: www.debt.org
- Internal Revenue Service: www.irs.gov
- Medicare: www.medicare.gov
- Social Security Administration: www.ssa.gov

Faith-Based Resources

- The Bible: It contains more than twenty-three hundred verses pertaining to debt, giving, planning, saving, guidance, God's provision, rest, worry, wealth, greed, and contentment, and 15 percent of what Jesus Christ said had to do with money or possessions. It can be purchased everywhere Christian books are sold.
- T. J. McBride Ministries: Empowering, Equipping, Enlightening and Encouraging Individuals to Serve and Glorify God: www.tjmcbride.org
- The Word for You Today: Connecting People with God's Word: www.wordforyou.com

Made in the USA
Columbia, SC
26 May 2019